Word Cravings

Bianca Grant

BookLeaf Publishing

India | USA | UK

To my husband Jon, thank you for seeing all the
ugly bits and thinking I'm beautiful because of
it.

ACKNOWLEDGEMENT

A special shout out to my Mother who told me that each one of these poems should be in a book after she read them. A special thank you to Sergio Jiminez for teaching me how to go back and edit to create stronger art.

PREFACE

When I became a mother, I lost myself. I have worked hard to get back to being an individual. Mother is my favorite title, but I am also a writer, artist, professional, and a friend. These are my thoughts as I worked through this journey back to me.

Wash and Dry

Home is at the sink where I do my thinking
I craft schedules while scrubbing plates
I envision my children's futures while
submerged to the wrist
In hot water
I build fortunes with steam
I wish on soap bubbles, not stars
Little hands slip sippy cups under my arm
I play music while I wash
Dancing to the tinkle of cutlery and my
children's giggles
My back aches with the weight of my baby on
my chest
I worry my way through the rent
Stress about health problems
Fret about the loss of jobs
While rinsing,
All those worries,
Down the drain.
My husband hugs me from behind and holds me
up
Lifts me onto the pedestal he's placed me
Right below God
So I don't mind doing the dishes
With feet planted in the house he's built
On hours of being away

While I am here sharpening the knives
I've laid out our dreams on cutting boards
Sanitizing any fear or expectations that might
linger
Rinsing leftover love from pots and pans left to
soak
I put home away to dry.

In the Morning

I cry in the morning
Before my kids can see
And I have to explain to them
What is wrong with me
I cry in the morning
While pushing through my pain
The tears are warm in the sunshine
And hidden by the rain
I cry in the morning
While planning out my day
All the things I want to do
All the thoughts I want to say
All the things I can't remember
All the pasts that I am mourning
To move forward toward the future
I cry in the morning

Today Love

Today I chose Love
That all-encompassing kind
I looked upon the little girl curled up inside my
heart reaching for comfort
And I loved her
Her flaws, her scars, her mistakes
I washed them away
Her tears I collected and poured out
Stand before me, child! So I can love you new
There are those that wish harm
For fears have twisted their face
Hold them up to the light and scream
I SEE THROUGH YOU!
Those discomforts that steal joy
I grasped tightly to my breast
I breathed with them until they released and flew
away like smoke
Yesterday is gone and tomorrow is not yet here
Flush out fear
Today I chose love.

A Moment

There is a moment in the morning,
When the fog of dreams lifts
Nightmares dissipate through unraveled
eyelashes
A moment of clarity
The sun peers in through the blinds
Searching for the person I could be
For a minute I forget
The weight of days before
That leaves me tangled in the sheets
That first waking breath fills
Lungs strained by expectations
Heart beating to the rhythm
Of itemized regrets
For a moment, in the morning,
The day stretches towards the future
And in the silence,
Only promise.

The Baby

Little voices are screeching, crying, giggling
Singing in that sing-song way
I don't hear a word they say
The baby is crying
Little hands are pulling my hair
Clawing at my clothes and skin
Are they trying to get back in?
The baby is crying
Little piles of toys underfoot
Dirty clothes pile up all around
I can't even see the ground
The baby is crying
My back is hurting
I haven't been sleeping
Overwhelmed by all the lists I've been keeping
The baby is crying
Does he want milk?
I know he's not wet
Why is the baby upset?
The baby is crying
My days are beginning to blur
Don't know if I'm coming or going
I'm alarmed at how fast my kids are growing
The baby is crying
Let me hold him.

Mushroom Cakes

My children mix imaginary cakes
They scrape empty bowls and fill empty plates
"Pass the mushrooms!", my daughter yells for
ingredients
"Mushrooms and apples and bananas" my son
calls out obedient
In a cake? The only thing they get right is the
eggs
And the mixing, mixing, mixing as I sip my tea
to the dregs
My newborn's lashes are laid flat with sweat
strapped to my chest
Breathing sweet milky breath into my neck,
hand tucked into my breast
We hold each other close as our hearts beat as
one
While my other two whisk up some fake kitchen
fun
I cook chicken while grease pops out of a pan
Cooking is the love language I understand
The kitchen fills up with warmth, love and
laughter
Full bellies and memories are what I am after
We turn up the music and dance around the table
Daddy comes to join in when he's able

I look at this family and can't believe they're
real
Gratitude and love is all that I feel.

Time

There's never enough time
I fight to keep the hours from sliding through my
hands
But the minutes seep through my fingers like
leaking water
Dripping dripping
I grasp each scattered task
A frightened bird vying for escape
My to do list becomes crumpled feathers
I'm trapped
In this endless cycle
Of half sung nursery rhymes
Repeating
As I shuffle each task to the next day endlessly
Each day extending
And at sunset I find
I have more to do the next day
Than when I started
What is this hourglass trick?
That never stops flipping
And I am left
Dizzy.

Thief

Death is a thief
That steals the way we would have loved
He sneaks in like a burglar
Uninvited
To take the words I wish I said away from me
He wears the face of a friend
To fool you
Into whispering more secrets, more promises
Death collects these
Like pressed flowers
I wake up and reach to call you
Death has taken your voice
Leaving just the memory of your voice in my
head
It tells me do not be angry
How can I not be?
You're gone now
And I am left with the ransacked space
Where death held me up
And snatched you from my heart

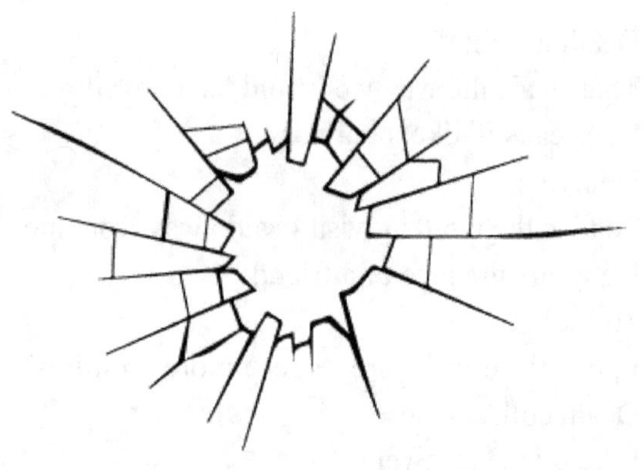

Gardening

For years I dug a hole
Fingernails crusted with clay
Not knowing what else to do

I choked on pieces of my soul
Not knowing what to say
Hiding from what was true

I searched the earth for my role
As more piled on by the day
It seemed my options were few

The darkness began to take its toll
I stretched roots out where I lay
Seeking sun, I clawed my way through

When I was ready to be whole
When the darkness couldn't stay
I grew.

Gentrified

DC is my home but I don't recognize her
You tried to bleach her skin.
It wouldn't take, so you slathered her in makeup
But her face doesn't match her neck.
She was fine the way she was.
Sure, she could have used a trim
And patches on some of her clothes worn
through, but they don't stitch like that anymore.
Instead you replaced the hand sewn with
polyester
And cut out what housed the memories of loved
ones that are ghosts now.
You tried to tame her but she stills breaks out in
gogo when you're not looking
She doodles protests in the corners of the
assignments you gave her.
You tarnished her! Shoved your hand up her
skirts, scooped out what she kept from you.
And told her she should be grateful.
You've pulled out by the roots, trees that still
carried my secrets.
I wanted to tell my children your mother loved
her, and her mother, and her mother before that.
You've put a pacemaker in and messed up her
rhythm.
Now her heart beats different.

DC was my home but now
I don't recognize her.

Ode to a Black Woman

Who are you to question my beauty?
Mother of nations.
My hair in the sun is like a burning bush from
which God speaks.
My skin, warm as fingers buried in earth
My curves, carved out by water on stone
My lips sing rhythms of hearts pounding in
breasts.
My laughter, a symphony of angel trumpets,
heralding the dawn.
I am Power. I am Passion. I am Love.
I am Infinite.
And in the darkness, I am what you seek
For I am Light.

Maybe Tomorrow

Maybe tomorrow
I have so much to do, so much to say
But I just can't do it today.
Maybe tomorrow
I'll wake up with all the words made clear
I'll be released from all fear
Maybe tomorrow
I'll have put the past behind me
I'll know how to find me
Maybe tomorrow
Today I'm tired, today I'm sad
Today I'm drowning in all the bad
But maybe tomorrow
I'll clean my room and wash my hair
I'll open up and finally share
Maybe tomorrow
I'll be glad I'm alive
I will do more than survive
Maybe tomorrow

Phoenix

I scream into the wind
Tears made of gas
This too shall not pass
The ropes of time still scarred around my neck
Each brown babe still born with lashes on their
backs
A stomach full of rage
And in nine months born a hot hope
For retribution
A phoenix
And I surrounded by flames consumed
Until this world is reborn.

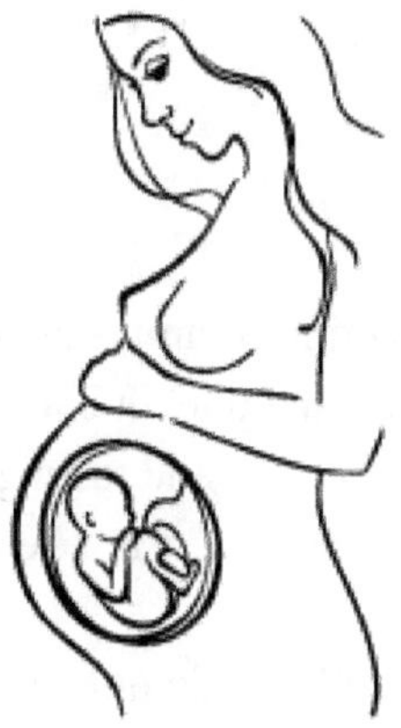

I Fell in Love

I fell in love
With eyes reflecting trauma shared
Cigarette blunt stained teeth bared
Lips lined with secrets and tasting of beer
I can touch you but you're not here
I fell in love
With a mirage of bravado unfurled
The weight lifted as toes uncurled
Moans gave way to sighs
Your declarations became lies
I fell in love
With living on the run
The escape into fun
The smoke screen rose with the sun
I fell in love.

Snoring

I love to hear my husband snore
His rumbling thunder
Rolls through the whole house
Comforting us all with his presence
Snoring means he's home
Snoring means we're safe
Snoring is a memory of growing up with my
grandparents
Who both snored
My husband snores and I'm 6 again
Listening to each roar and scratch
On Christmas Eve
As I waited for everyone to wake for presents
Snoring means my husband is resting
After working long hours to provide
Each rumble a testament
To every 5 am wake up call
Sometimes his snoring is too monstrous
Filled with the scratchy choke of stress
It wakes me up and I reach for him
Patting him gently at first
Then a loving shove
"You're snoring!" I mutter.
He reaches for me
Arms wrapped in love, trust, safety, and
Commitment

Pulls me closer
And stops snoring
For a moment
Until he drifts back into dreamland
And the thunder builds again.

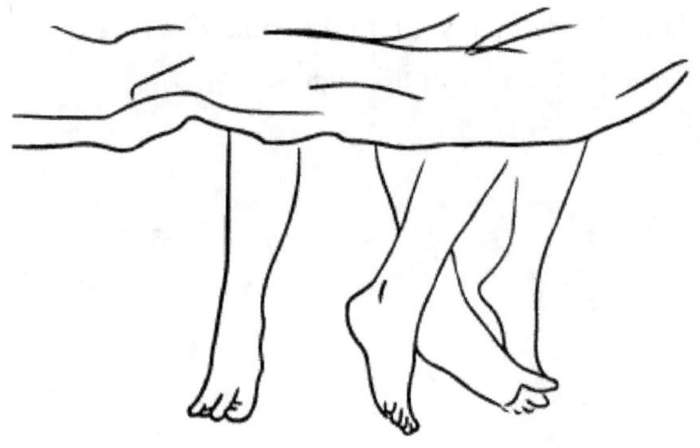

Mirror

Unfamiliar reflection
Daily push for perfection
Flaws under detection
Inner strength, the selection
Standing tall, an election
Who am I?
At the intersection
Of growth and imperfection
Feet facing the right direction
Affirm I am Love and Protection
A being built on connection
Confidence becomes an infection.

Home

I never knew what home was
I lived in fear, out of boxes and bags
Always moving from place to place
Never settling
I was searching for home
In rooms rented by the week
In the basements of other people's lives
They live and love above me
While I try to imitate a feeling I don't
understand
I never knew what home was
Whether home was the warmth of a mother's
embrace
All I knew was cold
I hurt myself searching for heat
Burning myself on false love
I was looking for home
In the quick ups and slow downs
Of powders and pills and bottles
I was looking for home in people
In their wet mouths and rough hands
In their empty, hollow words
I was looking for a home in the street
Hidden under cardboard
Buried inside change cups
I searched in Starbucks bathroom stalls

Loud voices demanded I search elsewhere
On the other side of the passcode door
I searched in motel rooms
In gang signs and handshakes
At the other end of jail phone calls
I searched for home in my job
Non-slip shoes and overtime
Each tip getting me one step closer
Until
I found home in a test
Two pink lines and a promise
That home would be the safety of my arms
I found home in a partner
Who loves me for me
No matter my flaws
I found home in a title
Mother, wife
Child of God
I found home

Doubt

The thoughts trip over themselves
Racing to the front of my mind
Leapfrogging one over the other
Until they reach the edge
And cascading over the cliff
Fall out of my mouth
I'm too much of this
I'm too little of that
I'm doing this wrong
IMPOSTER
The accusation screams behind my eyes
It sits squat and ugly in my stomach
I catch glimpses as I walk past mirrors
FAKE is hidden in the corners of my reflection
Like a threat
It clutters up the idea space
I have to clear out all the noise
And focus on the only voice that matters
In the chorus of voices chanting I can't do
anything
I listen to the one whispering I can.

Miracles

I forget miracles are miraculous
When the baby won't stop crying
And the toddlers won't listen
I forget I prayed for long nights of crying
To fill what could have been silence
A silence that would have reached in
And hollowed me
Instead I am filled
By cold baby feet pressed against my back
I forget miracles are miraculous
When there are toys on the stairs
And half eaten apples get thrown away
I had begged God for this
For little people who forget to put their pull-ups
in the Diaper genie
That first time
As they searched for a heartbeat that was not
there
I prayed for a miracle
And then six times double pink lines
Turned to blood, cramps, and tears
Each time I prayed, please and if only
Now I have thrown up milk on my work clothes
I have screams and giggles for breakfast
And nobody ever goes to bed
But miracles are miraculous
And I have three.

To the Person Called Mommy

To the person called Mommy
I see you
Heating up the same cold coffee
As your children pull you away again
You drink it cold.
Praying for energy to kick in to keep going
Because the baby keeps you up
And the worry
Are they breathing? Are they ok?
To the person called Mommy
I see you
Skipping that shower for the second day
As you bathe little feet and little hands
And top baby curls with bubbles
I know you ache for a moment to yourself
To wash your own hair
Cleanse the lingering smell of sour milk from
your skin.
To the person called mommy
I see you
Sacrificing.
The last of everything you have.
Your last bites, your last minutes,
Your last bits of yourself
To the person called mommy
I see you

Searching
For the image of yourself you once held
When you only answered to you
When you thought you were beautiful
I see you Mommy
You still are.

Word Cravings

I dream in metaphors
Imagine in verse and rhyme
When doing household chores
My heartbeat keeps the time

I scribble on receipts
Collect notes on my phone
I practice rhyming cheats
My vocabulary I hone

The thoughts that become ravings
The ideas that can't be found
Become the topic of word cravings
An experiment with sound

As I structure sentences, I have to take heed
Writing is not a hobby, but a need.